WOW Your Way To Wealth

The One Secret That Rich People Tell You That You've Never Heard

VISHAL MORJARIA

First edition published by Vishal Morjaria

www.WowYourWayToWealth.com

Copyright © 2014 Vishal Morjaria

Vishal Morjaria has asserted his right under the
Copyright, Designs, and Patents Act, 1988 to be
identified as the author of this work.

ISBN-13: 978-0-9575564-2-3

Reviews of WOW Your Way To Wealth

"Vishal wrote this book so that you can write yours. A superb demonstration of how you can transform an ordinary life into an extraordinary success story through words. WOW Your Way To Wealth is the key to unlocking the hidden potential that resides within each of us."

– Therese Barber,
Freelance Entrepreneur

"Engaging and enjoyable. Vishal opens up a whole new way of looking at wealth and success in WOW Your Way To Wealth. Here's a methodical and passionate approach that makes this book not only an easy read but also thought-provoking. It can turn you from being a reader to a writer."

– Leah Elliot,
Property Investor

"Vishal lays bare the mysteries of creating wealth with sheer ingenuity. There is nothing which will seem impossible after you read WOW Your Way To Wealth. Everything appears so simple and clear, you wonder why it didn't occur to you sooner. The secret to the book's appeal is its simplicity."

– Raymond Aaron,
New York Times Best Selling Author

ABOUT THE AUTHOR

Vishal wrote this book so that you can write yours.

The award-winning author currently lives in the UK but travels extensively across the world conducting seminars and workshops to help ordinary people discover their extraordinary potential, and transform their professional and personal lives.

Vishal transformed his life by turning the difficult experiences he had into positive life lessons. From struggling hard to make ends meet and suffering from clinical depression, Vishal transformed himself into an award-winning author, and a highly successful transformational coach and speaker.

Vishal believes that everyone has the right to lead a life that fulfils their potential and this is evident in the diverse lifestyles of the people he has inspired. The people who attend his workshops include aspiring entrepreneurs as well as disillusioned and dissatisfied professionals who want to see better results for their efforts.

FOREWORD

*D**ear extraordinary person,*
You have a secret power and this book shows you how to discover that secret.

WOW Your Way To Wealth contains a startling revelation. So brace yourself to be shocked.

It is very likely that reading it will produce a profound feeling of excitement that you can now make full use of the time and opportunity you have been given. It will also open your mind to dreaming big and doing even bigger things.

Do you know why you are earning far less money than you deserve? Do you know how you can make more money than you ever imagined? Do you know how very successful people do it?

Learn the answers to these questions in WOW Your Way To Wealth.

Pay careful attention to what Vishal presents in this important book. Your wealthy future depends on it.

Raymond Aaron
New York Times Best-Selling Author
www.2dayTycoon.com

(Raymond is the author of *Branding Small Business for Dummies* and *Double Your Income Doing What You Love*, besides many other bestselling books. He is known as the #1 success and investment coach, teaching people just like you how to use his goal setting strategies to change your life.)

DEDICATION

This book is dedicated to you, the reader of this book.
The idea for writing this book came to me when I attended a workshop conducted by Raymond Aaron. I wondered why I was not where I wanted to be despite my best efforts.

I had a moment of epiphany when I realised why. At that precise moment I knew I had to write this book. Not for me but for you.

This book is my way of acknowledging the importance of having a mentor and coach. The sheer amount of collective wisdom that I gained from interacting with my mentor, coach and now business partner, Raymond Aaron, changed my life for the better and I sincerely hope this book will change yours too.

Love
Vishal Morjaria

ACKNOWLEDGEMENTS

I express my thanks to Arun Raj, for clarifying my thoughts on paper and editing the book.

I also thank Therese Barber, for proofreading and eliminating embarrassing errors.

My family have coped and dealt with my eccentric personality during my time working on this book and supported my efforts without even knowing exactly what I was writing about.

None of this would have been possible without my coach, mentor and new found business partner Raymond Aaron, who has supported my success and has shown me the path to living my dream.

Finally, my most humble gratitude goes to the spiritual energy better known as the divine, higher source or god (which ever you feel most comfortable with) for allowing me this opportunity to make a difference in the lives of my fellow companions who come into contact with this book.

NOTE TO THE READER

The information, including opinion and analysis, contained herein is based on the author's personal experiences and is not intended to provide professional advice.

The author and the publisher make no warranties, either expressed or implied, concerning the accuracy, applicability, effectiveness, reliability or suitability of the contents. If you wish to apply or follow the advice or recommendations mentioned herein, you take full responsibility for your actions. The author and publisher of this book shall in no event be held liable for any direct, indirect, incidental or consequential damages arising directly or indirectly from the use of any of the information contained in this book.

All content is for information only and is not warranted for content accuracy or any other implied or explicit purpose.

CONTENTS

CHAPTER 1

Branding YOU

Be yourself. Everyone else is taken.

– Oscar Wilde

Do you see other people when you look at yourself? You are the most important person in your life. Do you agree with this view? If you have any doubts, go and take a good, long look at yourself in the mirror. What do you see? Did you see John Lennon? Richard Branson? David Beckham? Did you see Paris Hilton? Oprah? No, you didn't see any of these people, did you?

Hold that thought, right there! When I asked you, if you see someone else, you assumed it was just a rhetorical question.

Now, really, put down this book, get up and go look in the mirror. Yes, I know you did not do it the first time.

Let's face it. What you see is a reflection of yourself. But are you who you think you are? Are you who other people think you are? Do you know what others think about you or how they see you?

There is only one way to find out. Ask yourself these three questions:

- ☞ Who are you?
- ☞ What do you have to offer?
- ☞ Why should anyone care?

I will go first.

I am Vishal Morjaria. I am the award-winning author of 'Flab to FAB: The Holistic Guide to Effortless Weight Loss.' I am also the author of the book you are currently reading. I am who I am because I wrote these books. I wrote these books because I recognised and realised that I had knowledge, which I wanted to share with others so they could benefit by reading my books.

Now, it is your turn.

What is your response? You can say, 'I am (your name here) John Smith. I am 'a' _____' (your profession here—an accountant or a property developer or a businessperson or an entrepreneur). 'I am who I am because _____.' If you are an accountant, you may say something like, 'I am an accountant because I am good with numbers,' or 'I am a businessperson because I like to make money.'

But how does this distinguish you from other accountants or business people?

You need to go from being 'an' ordinary person to 'the' special or extraordinary person to create an impression. Otherwise, you are just another indistinguishable nail in the bin, just like the rest of them.

You see me as the authority on a particular subject because I wrote a book about it. Whereas, despite all the knowledge and wisdom you may have accumulated over the years, other people may, at best, perceive you as an expert. That is what other people see.

Do you see the difference?

If you had asked me to answer the three questions a few years back, my answers would have been quite similar to yours. The point is that there are a million or more people like you. You are not seeing a reflection of yourself in the mirror because the most important person now in your life is not you. It is the people around you.

Your reflection is the same as their reflection. You are not seeing someone special. You are seeing someone ordinary. The same as everyone else.

You are stuck in the same traffic jams, you stand in the same queues, you do the same thing, day after day, and at the end of the month you struggle to make ends meet. It is the same story all over again the next month, and the next year, and before you realise, it is too late to do anything about it.

At the moment you see someone who is just like everyone else. You are not seeing a reflection of yourself. You are seeing a reflection of everyone else.

FROM THE SEA OF SAMENESS TO THE ISLAND OF INDIVIDUALITY

You are in the Sea of Sameness. You may think that you are 'floating' or even 'swimming' in the Sea of Sameness but it's an illusion. This illusion is created by your own delusion that this is all you can be. You may be under the false notion that the Sea of Sameness is a comfortable place to be. It is not. You are slowly but surely diminishing your own individuality. You are merging with the background.

The truth is you are actually drowning.

But this should not be you, because you are, in fact, unique.

Look at successful people. What separates successful people from the rest?

Successful people are noticed. You do not see through them.

They attract attention and therefore, in turn, attract opportunities, people and wealth.

Success may mean many things to different people. However, what most of us would agree is that successful people do not just have material wealth; they are also happy and popular. In other words, they may have reached an extraordinary state of emotional, social and perhaps, even spiritual balance.

They are rarely upset when things do not go as expected. They feel at home, whether they are alone or in the company of friends, colleagues or acquaintances. They have found a place in the hearts and minds of people around them.

So, how do successful people achieve this state? They do so by attracting opportunities to utilise their talent and skills, connecting with other people and generating appreciation, goodwill and sometimes even praise for their efforts, which converts to a reliable means of income.

Successful people rise above the ordinary. They escape from the Sea of Sameness and establish their presence on the Island of Individuality.

If you want to be successful, you should attract more attention and more opportunities, which in turn will attract more clients and more income.

Therefore, the first step to WOW Your Way To Wealth is to create your own Island of Individuality. How do you do this? By Branding YOU as an individual, who is different from everyone else.

THE FOUR MOST POWERFUL WAYS OF BRANDING

When you buy something, you are buying either a product or the brand. You can buy an MP3 player. Alternatively, you can buy 'the iPod'. Similarly, you can buy a car or you can buy 'the ultimate driving machine.'

You could go on holiday to a beach resort, similar to the one you went to last year, or the year before that. Alternatively, you could go to some place extraordinary. You could climb Mt Fuji or Mt Kilimanjaro, or you could go scuba diving in the Maldives, or witness the great Serengeti Wildebeest migration.

You can do what others are doing, or you can do what few have done, or even what no one else has done.

Whether you are a plumber or a pianist, an executive or an entrepreneur, you need to create an aura of noticeability around you. You need to come out of the Sea of Sameness and establish your own Island of Individuality.

No amount of talent or hard work can match a deliberate and systematic approach to making your presence felt. You are an individual and if you want others to look at you in the same way, then you need to turn the spotlight on you.

We are under the impression that modesty is a virtue and that bragging about ourselves is not an attractive quality. This does not however mean that we merge ourselves into the crowd. You need to assert your individuality and raise the flag of your potential to perform. Only then will you gain opportunities to prove your capabilities.

Look at successful people around you. They are noticed. People trust them because they know they can deliver. Successful people are visible and they are credible.

You also need to acquire the qualities of visibility and credibility, if you want to become successful. How do you do this?

By branding YOU as an individual. By turning yourself from someone unknown and unnoticeable to a branded personality, an individual who stands apart, who just cannot be ignored, and when people meet you once, they will remember you forever.

So, what are the ways you can achieve this?

There are four simple yet powerful ways of establishing your personal brand. In the same way a product is developed into a brand that stands apart from other 'me-too' commodity products, you can also transform yourself into a brand. When you have your own personal brand, you will attract attention and opportunities to generate more income and wealth.

The Quadruple A Branding Battery

You may have heard of the battery that goes on and on. Do you realise that I do not even have to mention the brand name of the battery? Even without mentioning it, you already know which brand of battery I am talking about. This is exactly what the Quadruple A (or the AAAA) Branding Battery can do for you.

It can transform you from being anonymous, to being recognised and even being the subject of discussion and debate when you are not physically present.

So, here are the four powerful ways of branding yourself.

1. Branding by Association
2. Branding by Acknowledgement
3. Branding by Achievement
4. Branding by Authoring

Branding by Association

Branding by Association is the first step to establishing your individuality. When you associate yourself with well-known personalities, their credibility and visibility enhances your own personal brand. There are many ways you can associate, through networking, attending seminars and conferences or taking part in collaborative projects.

Let us say you are a Chartered Accountant and you know Robert Kiyosaki, the author of the "Rich Dad Poor Dad" books. Since you know Robert Kiyosaki, and have met him, you might be in possession of a picture of you and him hanging out. Consider the impact that you could have by putting this picture on your website, social networking profile or even a presentation.

When people associate you with a famous personality, they think that you are someone important. You immediately develop an aura of impact and influence. It is in many ways similar to the effect of turning on a spotlight. People start noticing you because you are no longer in the shadows. You are no longer drowning in the Sea of Sameness.

However, it is not easy nor is it possible for everyone to get the opportunity of being associated with someone who is well known. However, despair not, for there are other ways to brand YOU. That is why it is called the Quadruple A Branding Battery. There are three more ways you can gain visibility and credibility

Branding by Acknowledgement

Branding by Acknowledgement is asking people to express their opinion about you. It is not unlike a brand, book or movie getting good reviews from trusted critics. When people hear about you from a third person, it creates better credibility than you blowing your own trumpet.

Let us say you are a property consultant. When you say you are good at what you do, why should people believe you? Now, consider this. Have you helped some of the eminent and respected personalities in your city or town to find their dream houses? Have you helped well-known companies re-locate their offices to a more prominent and better-equipped business district? Can these former clients say so?

Imagine the mayor of your city stating on your business card or on your brochure or website, "John is my favourite property consultant." You will immediately be perceived as a very important and accomplished property consultant because you have a testimonial from none other than the Mayor, vouching for your expertise and abilities to deliver.

Do you see the visibility and credibility that you can gain through Branding by Acknowledgement? Now, it is not always very easy to get acknowledgements or testimonials from people who matter. This is especially the case if you are young and just starting your career.

So let us take a look at the third A in the Quadruple A Branding Battery.

Branding by Achievement

If you want people to take notice of you, then you have to demonstrate that you are better than average. To do so you have to rise above mediocrity and prove that you are the cream on the top, not just another me-too face in the crowd. You have to establish you superior credentials in any profession or industry.

Branding by Achievement is about announcing the milestones, awards and accolades that you have received. Even a small recognition bestows credibility on you in the eyes of potential clients or customers. So, do not ignore any achievement, however small. Leverage your achievements to strengthen your personal brand.

So for instance, a hitherto obscure movie suddenly shoots into the news and into people's awareness when it wins an award at a Film Festival. The Film Festival need not be an international event; it can even be a regional affair. Similarly, copies of a book, which has been gathering dust on the display shelves in bookstores, suddenly starts disappearing as readers vie to lay their hands on it when the writer is interviewed on radio or TV. It need not be someone as well-known as Oprah (that would be the ultimate compliment) but even an interview on the local radio show can sometimes do the trick.

So, how do you gain these achievements? By taking part in

industry related activities. However, as we all know, when it comes to industry related recognitions or awards, there are only one, two, or at the most, three winners. So, what do you do?

An achievement need not always be about coming first; it can also be about trying. Imagine for a moment you are a physical trainer. If you take part in a marathon even that can be portrayed and perceived an achievement.

If you came first in the marathon, that is great! But even if you only just finished running the distance of 42 km or 26.2 miles, that is still an achievement. Start with small achievements and then build your brand with bigger and better awards and accolades.

What if you do not know anyone famous and therefore Branding by Association is not possible? What if you do not have any testimonials and therefore Branding by Acknowledgement is out of the question? What if, achieving any level of recognition is not so easy in your professional area and so Branding by Achievement is not an option?

The good news is you still have another option. This is the fourth A in the Quadruple A Branding Battery.

Branding by Authoring

Branding by Authoring is by far the most underutilised and also, the most doable option. When you introduce yourself to people or when you give them your business card, do people say "Oh, well, thanks"?

Do you want them to instead say, "Wow"?

Try giving them a book instead of a business card. Not just any book. Give them a book that you wrote.

You have trouble writing your own CV, so how can you expect to write a book?

English isn't your first language, and wouldn't writing a book in English be way out of your league?

What can I write about? Why would anyone be interested in reading what I write?

Shouldn't I be working hard in my profession or my business, instead of writing a book?

What good can writing a book do? Will I make any money by writing a book?

I will leave a few blank lines for you to write any more excuses you can think of for not writing a book.

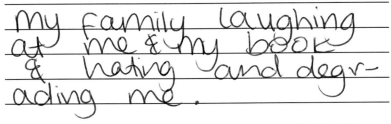

My family laughing at me & my book & hating and degrading me.

Now, if you have got all the excuses you can think of for not writing a book, let's look at how Branding by Authoring can catapult you from being an unknown, unnoticeable, nameless face in the crowd to someone who is visible and credible.

As Michael E Gerber, who is known as "the World's No. 1 Small Business Guru", and author of the bestselling book, 'Awakening the Entrepreneur Within' and the 'E-Myth' series of books, says, "Work on your business, not in your business."

If you had one day to work on your business, what would you do?

Would you go out and try to get new clients? Would you spend it on searching for courses to enrol in to get a new educational or professional qualification? Would you spend it on writing a new CV? Would you spend it on writing a new slogan or tagline for your business?

Or would you write a book?

Before you answer the question, I wish to relate an anecdote about my business partner and mentor, Raymond Aaron. For those of you who don't know, Raymond Aaron is the New York Times Bestselling author of eight books, which includes the popular, 'Double Your Income Doing What You Love,' 'Branding Small Business for Dummies' and two titles in the famous 'Chicken Soup for the Soul' series of books. In fact, he is the only author in the world to have written for both the 'Chicken Soup for the Soul' series and the 'For Dummies' series of books, which are arguably the world's two best-known nonfiction book brands or series.

But before he became an internationally renowned bestselling author and one of the most sought after speakers worldwide, Raymond was also an entrepreneur trying to create his Island of Individuality.

When he was 39, Raymond had a transformational experience. He lost his job, his wife divorced him and he was a hundred thousand pounds in debt. He then wrote a book, 'You can make a Million in Canadian Real Estate.' That was his first book and definitely not the last. Since, he did not know anyone who would endorse his book, he quoted himself on the cover, 'Security and happiness can be yours if you apply my principles for real estate success.'

By 41, Raymond's fortunes turned. He repaid his debts and became a millionaire. He gained visibility and credibility. He soon became one of the most sought after speakers and was invited to be one of the founding members of the Transformational Leadership Council (TLC), an elite group of authors, thought leaders, coaches, and other influential people such as Jack Canfield, author and creator of the 'Chicken Soup for the Soul' book series.

During this period, Raymond was flying on a business trip. The seat next to him was empty and it was a 5-hour flight. Raymond intended to quietly have a meal, watch two movies and relax. Just when he thought he could have some time to himself from his busy schedule as a much sought after speaker, another passenger came and sat next to his seat.

He said, 'Hi,' and Raymond had no option but to acknowledge and return the greeting. This is how the conversation went.

Co-passenger: "Hi, I am so and so."

Raymond: "Raymond."

Co-passenger: "So, what do you do?"

Raymond: "I help people like you double your income doing what you love."

Co-passenger: "Oh! Really? Do you have a card?"

Raymond: "No, I don't have a card."

Co-passenger: "You must be joking. You are in Business Class and you don't have a business card?"

Raymond: "No, I don't have a card but I have a book."

Co-passenger: "Wow! A book? You have a book? What's it called?"

Raymond: "Double Your Income Doing What You Love."

The guy couldn't believe what he just heard.

Co-passenger: "Do you have a copy?"

Raymond: "Yes, I have a copy."

Raymond always has a copy of his latest book. He takes out a copy of the book and gives it to his co-passenger. The co-passenger looks at the book and he is amazed. He wants Raymond to tell him how to do it (Double Your Income Doing What You Love).

Co-passenger: "We have 5 hours. Why don't you tell me what's in the book?"

Raymond: "Read the book."

Raymond wants to take a break from speaking and relax but the guy just won't let him.

Co-passenger: "Please tell me what's in the book."

Raymond: "I can but I'll have to charge you for that. Instead, I am giving you the book for free."

But the guy won't take no for an answer.

Co-passenger: "How much?"

Raymond thinks of a figure that may change his mind.

Raymond: "Five thousand dollars for a 50-minute hour."

Co-passenger: "Do you take Visa?"

Raymond: "We are on a plane . . ."

The guy takes out a damp napkin and writes down his credit card number, his name, the expiry date and the security number.

Raymond was giving him his book for free. He was not selling it. Yet, the guy wanted to pay him for sharing his wisdom.

You don't sell your book. Your book sells you.

Dr John Gray, author of 'Men are from Mars, Women are from Venus,' and a close friend of Raymond once told him, "I'd rather have a book than a PhD."

When Raymond asked him why a book is more important

than a PhD, Dr Gray explained. "If you are an author, the media would want to interview you. They would prefer an author to a Ph. D." Similarly, if you want to be taken seriously, you need to be perceived as an authority and not just as an expert.

If you have written a book, you must be important. If you have written a book, you have created something of value. Therefore, you must be someone who matters.

Your book acts as a catalyst and automagically catapults you from anonymity to being perceived as an authority.

Do you know what is it that the wealthy have that the others don't? It is of course, visibility and credibility. When you hear of someone who is in the top of their profession or business, you can clearly see that they are better than the rest and that they are trustworthy.

If you want to make your way from the crowd to the top 1% who have made it big, who possess not only wealth but visibility and credibility, then you have to command attention and be perceived as an authority.

When you write a book, people automatically perceive you as an authority.

Imagine sending a book that you have written along with your CV instead of sending just a CV. Can they afford not to call you for an interview? They cannot. Whether it is a job interview or a media interview, the moment anyone sees that you have written a book, they perceive you as a giant source of wisdom, an authority, someone worth meeting and talking with.

Imagine giving a book instead of handing over a business card. Will that person ever forget you?

You have a book in you and it is time to get it out of you.

BRANDING BY WOW

When people see a rainbow in the sky, they hold their breath. Why? It is because a rainbow is a rare occurrence, not an everyday affair. Similarly, you should create the impression that you are a rarity. In any field there are people who do the ordinary, and there are those who rise above.

How many people do you personally know, or have met, who have written a book? Is that a few, one or two or zero?

Nobody in my family before me has ever written a book. English is not even my first language. Despite all this, I wrote a book. So can you, if you know how. In this book, you will learn not just how to write a book, but how to create a WOW, and how to WOW Your Way To Wealth.

When a prospective client or business partner hears from you that you have written a book, they cannot believe it. When you then give them a copy of your book, they are in awe. They say WOW!

They now recognise that you are not just someone ordinary but someone who is exceptional. When you write a book, you go from floating in the Sea of Sameness to someone who is an authority, someone who has credibility and visibility because now you are on the Island of Individuality. After all, how often do you meet someone who has written a book?

This is how you create a WOW! You WOW your way into people's minds. Their awareness and their perception of you is transformed in that instant when you give them your book.

You don't sell your book. Your book sells you.

It is not what you think about yourself that matters. It is what your prospective clients think about you that matters.

A brand is more than just a name, a logo, colours or a slogan or tagline. It is an identity that comprises all these, and the consumers awareness or perception about the brand.

The first question that a potential customer asks is, have I heard about it or seen it before? This is awareness. A brand that has better visibility has greater brand awareness in the market place. Visibility is gained through advertising and sending out positive and powerful marketing messages.

The second question is, can I trust this brand? Is this a quality brand? This is credibility. A brand that has established itself as a popular brand through association, acknowledgement or achievement gains credibility. However, a brand that has a book written about it has much more to offer. It is a brand that has the power to transform.

Think Apple. Think Starbucks. Think Virgin Airlines.

Just look up books about any of these brands and you will find at least a dozen of them on Amazon. Whether it is a biography of Steve Jobs or a book written by Howard Schultz or Richard Branson or books about different aspects of the brand, you will find plenty of reading material.

Why? These brands are worth writing about.

Are you worth writing about as an individual? Unless, you are famous or have done something extraordinary, no one will write about you but that does not mean you cannot write a book on your own.

It does not have to be a memoir or an autobiography. In fact, it should not be. Very few people are likely to be interested in reading your memoirs unless you are famous or notorious. However, you can still write a book, a non-fiction, which makes people sit up and take notice of you as a person and as an author.

You know more than your reader about something. It could be a series of insights or experiential wisdom that you have gained. It will transform you from being perceived as someone who is ordinary, to someone who is an authority.

The Ladder of Wealth

There is a method of attracting opportunities to create wealth. It involves understanding the process of going from someone who is invisible and floating in the Sea of Sameness, to someone who confidently stands out on their Island of Individuality. This process follows the rungs on the Ladder of Wealth.

There are four rungs on the Ladder of Wealth.

1. Invisibility.

2. Visibility.

3. Credibility.

4. Wealth.

Going from being invisible, from being another drop in the Sea of Sameness to someone who is substantial and trustworthy is a long journey for most people. That is because they fail to understand the key to Branding by WOW.

Branding by Authoring is the most underutilised and also the most easily doable method of creating a WOW and establishing your own Island of Individuality.

Sure, writing a book is not easy. But nor is it impossible. This book will show you that it is possible to write a book in no time.

It took Raymond Aaron four years to write his first book and a lesser number of years for his next and so on. It progressively gets easier with each new book that he writes. Now, he can write a very good book in very little time and he can even teach you how to write a book in just 10 hours. It took me less than a year to write my first book. It took me much less time than that to write this one.

There is a systematic method to writing a book. If you follow the method, it is possible to write a book in 10 hours, if you want to.

Now, if you had 10 hours to work 'on' your business, what would you do?

That is right, write a book. No more procrastination. No more doubts. Create a complete transformation with your own book. Not just a transformation in how people perceive you, but a transformation in someone's life every time they read your book. When you write a book, people perceive you as an authority.

When you write a book, you go from the bottom rung on the Ladder of Wealth, Invisibility, straight to the top rung, Wealth. Why? A book enables you to gain Visibility and Credibility, all at once.

To know more about branding, visit www.WowYourWayTo Wealth.com.

REFLECTIVE QUESTIONS

☞ What did you learn from this chapter?

- Anything is possible.
- Inspired by Raymond.
- Your book creates well.
- You are an authority when you have a book written by you.

☞ What did you most like about this chapter?

Raymond's Story.

- It's not important how you see yourself, but how others see you.

☞ How will you apply what you have learnt from this chapter?

- I too can do the same.
- Writing a book will make people see me as an authority.

NOTES

• Write a book that transforms people's lives.

CHAPTER 2

Transactional Vs Transformational

Everyone thinks of changing the world but no one thinks of changing himself.

– Leo Tolstoy

Every day you interact with people. At work, you interact with colleagues or business partners or customers, and in your personal relationships, you interact with family members or friends.

Do you imagine yourself ever making a difference in their lives? Or do you just treat every interaction as a routine everyday affair?

You transact or exchange information when you interact with someone.

Every interaction is an action. Most of your actions are intended to fulfil a need. So for instance, you go to buy groceries because you need to eat, drink, brush your teeth and do your laundry.

Therefore, you may go to a shop and buy things such as fruit, vegetable, meat, water, juice, toothbrush, toothpaste, dental floss, detergent and so on.

What are you doing?

You are merely going through the motions required to live or exist. You are not doing anything out of the ordinary. You are just doing what everyone else does. You are just doing what is expected of you.

This is doing the Transactional.

You exchange your time, effort and money for material or products that you need to live.

It does not create any waves. It is not hard to do. It is normal. It is ordinary.

Some may even say it's boring but it's necessary. It is something you have to do every day. You have to sleep then get up, eat, drink, brush your teeth, go to work, play, meet people, and at the end of the day, go back to bed.

You have to do this day in and day out. There is no way you can avoid doing most of it.

It's routine.

Nobody expects you to climb a mountain or swim across the English Channel. However, if you did do the unexpected, then you are doing something out of the ordinary.

You are doing something Transformational.

You are making a splash. You are creating waves. You are getting other people's attention.

This is what gives you the potential to raise yourself from living an ordinary life like most people. The potential exists in all of us. What you do with the potential is what separates the extraordinary from the ordinary.

You can rewrite your CV many times. No matter how many times you rewrite it, you are still doing something ordinary. But if you wrote a book and sent it along with your CV, then isn't that extraordinary?

Imagine how it can transform your potential future employer's perception of you.

This is transformational.

You need to do the transactional because it's necessary. It's inevitable. But when it comes to doing something transformational, it is optional. You choose how your life will be.

Will it be ordinary? Or will it be extraordinary?

You cannot avoid the transactional. You have to do it because it is required. However, in the process we tend to ignore the transformational and lose sight of what is really possible.

Do you need to do something transformational? That's an answer only you can provide.

You cannot afford not to do the transformational if you want to be healthy, wealthy and successful. By being transformational, you attract better people in your life, attract better and more clients in your business, attract more opportunities and create more wealth, and also have the opportunity to transform not just yourself and your life, but the lives of the people around you.

By doing the transformational, you have the opportunity to transform the world around you. You can make it a better place. You make a positive impact and leave a lasting impression.

YOU DON'T SELL YOURSELF BY SAYING "I AM AN ORDINARY PERSON."

When someone asks you what it is that you do you do for a living, you generally tend to say that you are 'an' accountant, 'a' designer, 'an' executive, 'a' doctor, 'a' mechanic, 'a' manager or even 'a' CEO.

That is, you say that you are just one among a million other accountants, designers, executives, doctors, mechanics, managers and CEOs. You are just another drop in the ocean, another grain of sand on the beach, or just another ordinary person.

But you are an individual. So demonstrate your individuality when you say who you are.

You could be 'the' accountant who helps his or her clients save money.

You could be 'the' designer who created 'the' _____ logo or 'the' _____ poster.

You could be the executive who gets things done in the most efficient and pleasant manner.

You could be the doctor who enables a quick recovery through holistic treatment.

You could be the mechanic who guarantees better performance when he or she repairs something.

You could be the manager who improves productivity in people.

You could be the CEO who multiplied a company's revenues.

Every person, including you, has to create the role they play. If you do not create your own character, you will be a nameless, faceless, and perhaps even voiceless extra in your own life.

You can't play a supporting role in your own life, can you? No. You are reading this book because you want to define your own personality with a clear vision and conviction of what it is that you can do, that others cannot. You want to differentiate yourself from others.

When you go to a supermarket, you choose brands that appeal to you. In spite of the fact that there are a dozen or more choices, you choose a particular brand. Why? That's because this particular brand possesses visibility and it has established credibility among a sea of other me-too brands.

So don't say, 'me too.' Don't say 'I am 'a' someone' or 'I am ordinary.' Say 'I am 'the' person who makes a difference to people's lives because I do the extraordinary.'

You'll never get anywhere by imitating or copying others or being another face in the crowd. You have to stand out, and to stand out you need to create visibility and credibility by offering the promise to deliver something out of the ordinary.

You don't sell yourself by being ordinary. When people see you as someone extraordinary, they will be interested in you.

You suddenly become visible and you engage their attention,

and thereby have the opportunity to gain their trust and establish credibility.

Transactional exchanges are a part of your life. You cannot avoid the mundane tasks but you should not let your energy get bogged down by just doing these. You should find the time and the strength to do the extraordinary.

Then you make people sit up and take notice of you. You can even make a difference in other people's lives. But in order to do so, you need to first make a difference in your own life. You need to see yourself as someone who is special.

If you don't see the spark in your own self, how can you illuminate your presence when you step on the stage?

CHANGE THE WAY YOU SEE YOURSELF.

Do you see the difference between yourself and the rest of the people around you? Do you see the potential to do something extraordinary and transformational?

If you consider yourself as someone ordinary, do you think others will treat you any differently?

It's raining outside and you are in your office or at home. Imagine you're on the third or fourth floor. You open the window and look outside. What do you see?

Numerous umbrellas are bobbing up and down the sidewalk.

They are all nondescript. They all look the same. You can't tell one from the other, can you? One of them could be you. So how do you differentiate yourself?

You can carry an umbrella which is a unique colour.

An optical phenomenon makes a rainbow appear in the sky. But are they real or an illusion?

Rainbows are real, if you realise that white light, or light as we ordinarily see, it consists of seven colours, which are merged. Rainbows are unreal, if you don't know or don't believe in the individuality of each colour.

You can carry a uniquely coloured umbrella, but will other people believe the optical phenomenon?

Are you trying to creating an illusion because you don't really believe in your uniqueness? A superficial attempt to create a personality that doesn't fit you, will not fool others.

If you think you are not a champion, you cannot credibly carry that umbrella.

You have to know and believe in your heart that you are a champion.

Stop looking at yourself as others see you and start looking at yourself as you would like to be seen by others. Unique, not ordinary.

Only when you change your own perception of yourself, can you expect others to change how they see you.

YOU ARE UNIQUE. DON'T PRETEND TO BE ORDINARY.

In order to understand how innovation can change perceptions, let's look at some popular brands that changed the way consumers behaved or experienced something which was ordinary into something extraordinary.

In the world of personal computers, Apple chose to be different. You either buy a PC or a Mac. The PC is nondescript even though you have many brands to choose from. Apple innovatively transformed all the elements to make it a unique experience, from the design and hardware to the operating system and the software applications.

Apple similarly transformed the way people consume music. You either bought an MP3 player or you bought an iPod. Nobody refers to a Macintosh as a PC or a MacBook as a notebook or laptop. Similarly, you don't refer to an iPod as an MP3 player.

You also don't call an iPad, a tablet.

'The' MacBook, 'the' iPod and 'the' iPad are examples of the transformational. They changed the way people used 'a' PC, 'an' MP3 player or 'a' tablet.

Similarly, you either go to a café to get a coffee or you could go to Starbucks.

It's not just your professional aspect that you transform by doing the transformational. It's your life.

You go from being someone who is good at his or her job to someone who is exceptional. You go from being an ordinary son or daughter to being someone who is held up as an example by other parents.

You go from being invisible to being highly visible. You go from being ignored to being sought after.

To learn how to consistently make a transformational impact, visit www.WowYourWayToWealth.com.

REFLECTIVE QUESTIONS

☞ What did you learn from this chapter?

> • you must first change
> yourself first.
> • Be extroardinary &
> transformational. Don't
> ever be average!

☞ What did you most like about this chapter?

> • you must different-
> iate yourself from
> others. Stand out!
> • Be unique not
> ordinary.

☞ How will you apply what you have learnt from this chapter?

> • you have to know &
> believe that you are a
> CHAMPION!
> • From invisible to
> visible.

NOTES

CHAPTER 3

The Five Pillars of Wealth

Rich people have small TVs and big libraries, and poor people have small libraries and big TVs.

—Zig Ziglar

What is wealth? It means many things to many people but what does it mean to you?

Is it lots of money in the bank, or gold and silver stashed in a secret locker or treasure chest? Is it a big house, or many big houses and lots of big cars, TVs and very small smartphones and tablets?

Or is it freedom that comes from knowing that you don't have to worry about what you can afford and what you cannot.

Everything comes with a price. So does wealth.

If you do not have your own definition and understanding of what wealth means, then even if you have lots of money, you are still poor in many ways because you don't know what wealth means to you.

You cannot use someone else's yardstick to measure your

wealth. You need to have your own standards to benchmark what it is that differentiates being rich from being poor.

This may come across as too philosophical an argument, but wealth is essentially a metaphysical concept rather than a material concept.

Wealth on its own is worthless. It's what wealth can do for you, or what you can do with it, that makes it worthwhile or even valuable.

Gold is valuable but you cannot build bridges or make heavy machinery with gold. To make machines or to build utilitarian structures, you will need stronger metals like iron and steel or some sort of alloy that combines the qualities of strength, flexibility, malleability and resilience to withstand wear and tear. With gold, you can make ornaments and decorations, but you can't build structures. However, you can use the value of gold to buy the right kind of materials required to build bridges or industries.

Gold on its own is worthless. It's the value that is attributed to gold or silver that makes it valuable. This value goes up or down according to political, business, technological and economic events. The value is, if not arbitrary, at least not in our control.

So, like everything else, wealth also comes with a price.

The important thing to remember is that the price you pay for creating wealth should not prevent you from enjoying its benefits.

What does wealth mean to you?

Since I wanted to have a holistic view of wealth, I asked people from different walks of life what wealth meant to them. I also researched philosophers, wealthy and successful businesspeople, scientists and inventors, artists, musicians and all kinds of leaders and influential people, to see what their views were and to understand the true meaning of wealth.

During my research, I came up with five key aspects of wealth that repeatedly resonated among most people. These were Health, Finance, Relationships, Spirituality and Giving Back.

Of course, the order in which I mention them is not important. I think each aspect is equally important. And I realised that only by striking a balance between each of these aspects would you be able to have a happy, successful, and fulfilling life.

So, for instance, even if you were able to achieve tremendous financial wealth but in the process neglected your health, then all that money you earned will be of no use to you in the graveyard. Or if you ignored, antagonised or repelled the people who truly love you while you were busy in your pursuit of financial wealth, you may end up a sad and lonely person with no one to share the wealth you have created.

That's why I think it is important to examine all five aspects of Health, Finance, Relationships, Spirituality and Giving Back in the context of wealth.

The true meaning of how we perceive wealth lies within each of us.

What wealth means to me need not be what wealth means to you. It's something that you have to explore and find out for yourself through introspection and examining what kind of wealth it is that you want, why it is important to have wealth, and how you are going to be wealthy.

Creating your wealth is a journey of discovery.

However, like on any journey, there are a few general pointers or direction signboards, which will serve you well in your quest to create wealth.

One important thing to remember is this book is not about just creating wealth in a transient manner, but it is about enabling you to create wealth for life.

That's why I think that it is important to enjoy not just the wealth you create but also the process of creating this wealth. That's why this book is called WOW Your Way To Wealth.

HEALTH: IT IS THE SOURCE OF YOUR ENERGY.

There is no denying that health is a primary factor in creating wealth and in enjoying the benefits of the wealth you create. You need to take care of your health because it is health that provides you with the energy that you need in order to create wealth.

According to a quote attributed to the Dalai Lama, "Man sacrifices his health in order to make money. Then he sacrifices money in order to recuperate his health." Now, this is not very hard to understand.

Most people become so focussed on their jobs, or on the business, they forget everything else and pour all their energy into creating wealth. What they don't realise is the source of all their passion and energy is their health.

When it comes to health, there are two areas you need to look at. One is your physical health and the other, your mental health.

I cannot emphasise enough the importance of maintaining your mental health because neglecting it can lead to severe psychological complications. It is very easy to overlook a weakening of your mental health because signs of deterioration in this area are not immediately noticed. Just as you should take care of your physical health with exercises, you need to keep your mental health active and invigorated through mental exercises.

I personally underwent a lot of anguish and trauma when I lost control of my mental health for about a year and a half. I fell into a deep, dark hole mentally and psychologically because I could not control the negative thoughts in my mind, and I went into severe bouts of depression and mood swings. When you are in such a state of mental stress, confusion reigns and it is very difficult to differentiate between what is correct and what is not. It becomes a mental prison. If you don't take steps to relieve yourself from stress and consciously direct your thoughts towards positive thinking, it is possible for anyone to end up in a mental prison without realising it.

It's not easy to admit that you were once crazy, but the fact is that I was. I still am a little bit crazy, but now it is in a good way because now I know I am in control of my mental faculties and am fully aware of what I am thinking. Now I can keep track of my emotional and physical reactions.

It is important to nurture and nourish your mental health just like you would your physical health. One of the first things you should start practicing is meditation. Meditation is nothing but spending quality time with your thoughts, allowing them to form and then analysing and interpreting them. However, in order to examine your thoughts, you first need to empty your mind of all thought and then allow your thoughts to pass through naturally. You can take the aid of many online audio and video tips to meditate or you can attend a coaching class to learn the basics.

The second thing is to concentrate on your breathing. Find a quiet place, room or corner and focus on your breathing. This will help you to clear your mind of confusion and bring clarity to your thoughts. Paying attention to your breathing is quite similar to meditating and is in some ways a form of meditation.

Another way to nourish your mental faculties is to read. Read something that you enjoy whether it is autobiographies, biographies, fiction, memoirs or books on subjects that you are interested in. Another important form of mental exercise that you can perform is solve puzzles or play games. This could be anything that interests you such as crosswords or Sudoku or playing board games like Scrabble or Chess. It has been observed that playing board games stimulate the cognitive abilities of thinking and reasoning.

When it comes to your physical health, you need to consider two important aspects, nutrition and exercise.

I attribute 80% importance to nutrition and 20% to exercise. Nutrition is important because you are what you eat. Instead of following complicated diets, you can apply some simple rules to ensure that you receive ample nutrition to maintain a healthy and energetic lifestyle.

Firstly, eat food that is natural and alive. This means you consume more fresh fruits and raw vegetables. As much as possible, try to get organically grown fruits and vegetables because these provide safer and more natural sources for most of the nourishment your body needs. Also, organic fruits and vegetables will ensure you reduce consumption of any harmful chemicals.

The second rule is to avoid food that will make you fat because then it contributes to low self-esteem and leads to a lethargic lifestyle. How to know what to avoid? Use the BRPP formula. That's 'B(u)RPP' without the 'u', where B stands for Bread, R for Rice, P for Pasta and the second P for Potatoes. This is particularly useful when you are trying to lose weight and it also enables you to cultivate healthy lifestyle habits for the long term.

As a physical fitness trainer and coach, my advice to you regarding exercise, is to focus on activities that you enjoy. This will ensure that you not only do them regularly but you will also be able to continue doing them throughout your life thereby bringing you immense benefits in terms of the quality and the quantity of your life. So whether it is biking, hiking, running, swimming, going to the gym, attending Pilates or Yoga classes, whether it is indoor activities or outdoor activities, you need to discover what appeals to you.

Most importantly, the activity should encourage natural movement of your body and you should not feel that you are being forced to do it. That's when exercise becomes torture and unbearable. It should be enjoyable and only then will you benefit. Actually, if you do it right, you need to perform any exercise only 3 times a week and as little as 20 minutes a day. The important thing is to sweat and allow the pores of your skin to flush out the toxins and waste.

FINANCE: HOW SMALL CHANGES CAN BRING SUBSTANTIAL RETURNS.

Finance is about money. It is about earning more money than you spend so that you can create wealth. Why create wealth? So that you can do all the good things that you want to do with the money that you have.

But finance is not just about money. It is also about your attitude towards it.

It's a sad fact that most people think that money or making money is a bad thing. You should realise that money by itself is not a bad thing. It's what you do with your money that counts. If you think that money is not important then there is no way you will be able to create wealth because mentally you have put up a barrier to creating wealth. You have already decided to be poor.

Consider this important fact. Almost 3% of the people in this world control 97% of the wealth. Instead of looking at this as an unfair and disheartening fact of life, you should be able to spot the opportunity in it. The bottom of the pyramid is overcrowded while there is room and opportunity for you to move up the pyramid.

Why do you work? To earn money in order to put food on the table, provide for yourself and your family, to pay the rent and bills and in order to survive.

Do you want to just survive or do you want to live a fulfilling life?

Most people will publicly acknowledge the need to make money, but deep in their hearts they think and believe that money is unimportant or even that it is the source of evil. This is a result of many years of conditioning caused by a combination of moral, philosophical, religious and social discourse and education. You have been told that money is the root cause of all evil and therefore you have unconsciously created within you a barrier to creating wealth.

You have been brainwashed and you need to use your powers of reasoning and thinking to understand why you are not making enough money, despite working very hard.

That's because you are in denial. You either think money is bad and therefore you don't need it, or you think that making more money will turn you into an evil person.

You need to look on the brighter side. If you had more money, think of all the things you could do to make this a better world. Of course, you can always say that you don't need money to do good deeds but you have to realise that if you have wealth then you are in a better position to do the things you want to do. Wealth brings you the power and resources to do something transformational instead of the transitional, to do something extraordinary instead of just surviving.

When you work very hard and do not get the rewards you expect, you become stressed and tired. This is when you become confused and unhappy, which leads to a deterioration in your health and in your relationships. You start to lose control of your life.

What you should do when you find yourself in such a situation is to simply take stock. If you are working for someone else and if you believe that you are not getting paid what you deserve, you simply need to find another job that will pay you what you think you truly deserve. This is important for regaining your self-esteem and self-confidence. However, instead of exchanging one bad job for a slightly better one, have you considered working for yourself? Have you considered becoming an entrepreneur?

Entrepreneurship is nothing but venturing on a journey into uncharted territories. If you have a roadmap, you will not lose your way. In business terms your roadmap is your plan or strategy. Do you have one?

According to Brian Tracy, the author of 'The 21 Success Secrets of Self-Made Millionaires,' it's a question of putting into practice some very simple steps to become a millionaire. There are more self-made millionaires than you imagined and every day, there is someone who is embarking on this journey. It could be your journey, too.

A few years back, I was in a situation where I was not making much money despite working very hard. Perhaps, you are today in a similar situation.

It was then that my coach, mentor and business partner, Raymond Aaron asked me if I had a technique or strategy to make money. I realised I didn't.

I was on the bottom rung of the ladder of wealth. I was invisible. Perhaps that's where you are today.

I realised that to create wealth I needed to climb the next two rungs. Gain visibility and credibility. How to do it? By branding myself, and what's the best way to brand your own self? As I mentioned before, it's through Branding by WOW.

I wrote a book and the rest is, as they say, history. In fact, I am writing my future and creating my life with every word I write, every action that I take. You can also brand yourself by learning the technique of Branding by WOW.

Writing a book could be your ticket to a new life, of being able to afford to do the things that you've always wanted to do.

It is however important to do it the right way and this book will put you on the right track so that you can WOW Your Way To Wealth.

To learn tried and tested techniques to writing a book, visit www.WowYourWayToWealth.com.

RELATIONSHIPS: COMMUNICATE AND CO-OPERATE INSTEAD OF CONTROLLING.

Relationships are important. Relationships define a person. Good relationships can provide tremendous impetus in your journey towards success and creating wealth.

Take for instance, your relationships at work. If you have better relationship with your colleagues, business partners, clients or customers, then you will have more opportunities to create wealth. Similarly, personal relationships, whether they are with your family members or with friends, can immensely contribute to your emotional and physical wellbeing, thereby energising you to pursue your passion.

The key to good relationships lies entirely within you. Only you have the power to make your relationships work. I have found that there are three simple guidelines that you can follow to create good relationships. They are Communication, Control and Co-operation.

Communication is the first step to establishing a link between two people in a relationship. Take for instance marriage. When there is no proper communication between husband and wife, it leads to misunderstandings, creating a widening chasm of mistrust driving potential life partners away. The same is the case with people at work, between a manager and an employee, or between an entrepreneur and a client, or an executive and a customer.

All communication should establish a one-to-one connection.

The key to this is to relate to the person you are communicating with and understanding what it is that he or she expects from you. In order to do this you need to listen first to what they are saying. Effective communication begins with actively listening to what the other person is saying. So pay careful attention to what they say to you.

Control is overrated.

You cannot control other people. The more you try to the less you will be able to. The only person you can control is yourself. It is when one person tries to control another person, that resistance and resentment starts to build.

Once a person decides to resist your efforts to control their actions or behaviour, you might as well be trying to go through a wall. In fact, it's not unlike hitting your head against a wall, the only result will be a perpetual migraine. So stop trying to control others. Instead, try to influence them by setting examples or explaining or even demonstrating your point of view.

The more you try to control, the less you will have opportunities to influence and the more you try to influence, the less you will need to control.

Finally, the most productive way to make the most out of relationships is to be co-operative.

In a relationship between two people, each person should have an equal benefit that matches what the other person is getting from the relationship. Put simply, there should be mutual give and take.

This is possible only if both parties in a relationship take steps to understand and help the other person.

So for instance, consider two people at work. Each has his or her own responsibility. One of them has the responsibility of calling customers while the other is supposed to write to them. What if each of them does not like what they are supposed to do? Now, it's possible that the person who is supposed to call enjoys writing e-mails while the person who is supposed to write e-mails prefers to make telephone calls. If they exchanged their responsibilities, they would be happier and they would have established a bond of co-operation.

I also would like to share with you a formula that can ensure that your relationships do not fail.

It is D+E=D. What does it stand for?

Dependency + Expectation = Disappointment.

It may appear very simple and hard to believe but let me demonstrate how it works.

A boy and girl are in a romantic relationship. The boy gives the girl chocolates and flowers every time they meet. After a few occasions, the boy stops bringing chocolates or flowers whenever they meet. The girl is likely to be disappointed. Why? It's because the boy has created a sense of dependency and expectation in the girl to receive flowers and chocolates.

Now, the girl invites the boy over to her place for a home-cooked dinner. The boy is looking forward to it. He expects a great meal and a wonderful ambience. His having a good time is dependent on the girl being able to meet his expectations. When the boy arrives at her place on a Friday evening, the house is in an absolute state and she has not yet prepared the meal. He is naturally, disappointed.

Do you see now, how you can use the formula to avoid disappointment in your relationships? The key is to avoid becoming dependant and not to have unrealistic expectations, and to be prepared for disappointment. This way, each partner will be able to stay stable, steady and grounded in reality.

You have the power to influence your relationships by learning to communicate, relinquishing control over others and by having control over your own self, and by co-operating with others.

SPIRITUALITY: FIND YOUR LIFE'S MEANING AND PURPOSE.

Your real worth lies within you. It is waiting to be utilised and if you don't use it, it will go to waste.

The sad part is, if you are not aware of what's within you, you will never have the opportunity to realise your full potential. In order to nurture your inner potential, you need to stop looking at what's outside and recognise what's inside you.

I'd like to use a metaphor to explain this. Consider a seed. It's small and mostly invisible, and often overlooked. But is it insignificant? I am sure you would agree that it is not. It is the tiny seed that produces a tree.

Yet it is often ignored because we generally only see the visible manifestation of the seed. The leaves, the branches, the fruits, the trunk of the tree and even the roots underneath the ground—we acknowledge their presence, but we do not pay much attention to the seed. We know the seed once existed. We know that the seed was the main cause for bringing the tree into existence, but when we look at the tree, we think the seed no longer exists. Why? We think it is no longer required.

The seed is like your soul. It existed before you were born but now that you have a form in the shape of a human being, you think that it no longer exists.

You have a body. You have eyes. You have ears. You have a nose. You have hands. You have legs. Do you have a soul?

Do you say, 'I am my body?' No, you say, 'This is my body.'

Similarly, you don't say, 'I am my eyes, my ears, my nose, my hands or my legs.' You say 'These are my eyes, my ears. This is my nose, these are my hands and these are my legs.'

When you say you are a human being, you are aware of the 'human' aspect. It is what you can see and therefore believe as existing. It is the visible, the tangible part of you.

What you forget about or don't notice is the 'being' aspect in the 'human being.'

When you say, 'I am . . .' that's what you are referring to. You are referring to the being within you, your soul. You may call it whatever you want to—soul, spirit, energy, consciousness, god—but you can neither prove, nor deny its existence.

The soul, unfortunately, cannot be separated from your body and placed in a test tube to be studied. That's why there will always be a sceptical part within each of us, which will question the existence of the soul. It is inevitable.

However, denying the existence of our soul is to deny our true purpose. It creates a sense of ennui and prevents us from realising our full potential. So, why is it important to find meaning or purpose?

I would like to quote Shakespeare's Hamlet, "There is nothing either good or bad, but thinking makes it so." There is a profound insight in this statement.

If you think something exists, then it does. If you think it doesn't, then it doesn't. So, even if you have all the wealth in the world, but are not content, or you do not know what to do with it, then all the wealth you have is of no use because you are incapable of appreciating it.

On the other hand, if the whole world seems against you, but you believe in your heart that you possess value, then you will realise that value and convert it into wealth.

Steve Forbes said, "The real source of wealth and capital is not material things, it is the human mind, the human spirit, the human imagination and our faith in the future."

Dwell on these words.

In conclusion, I'd like to narrate a parable and also provide some advice.

There was a princess who had inherited an exquisite necklace of pearls. She was very proud of this valuable possession and she never missed an opportunity to wear them. It so happened that there was a great ball to which she was invited. The event was hailed to be one of the most important occasions, because all the 'who's who' of the time and place would be present.

On the day of the event, as the princess was getting ready for the party, she suddenly realised that her precious pearl necklace was missing. She looked high and low and she couldn't find it. She called all her family members and every member of the household to look for it. They also couldn't find it. She was depressed and dejected. She decided that she wouldn't go to the party because she didn't have her prized possession.

She was inconsolable and everyone finally left her alone to cry. At last, when she had finally exhausted the tears of sadness that welled up inside her, she raised her face to wipe away the tears. She looked in the mirror and saw that the thing she was looking for all along was around her neck.

You may not believe in your soul. Or you may just have lost sight of it. Or you may be looking for meaning and purpose in your life. I was in a similar situation and I found guidance and solace in an organisation called the Brahma Kumaris. It is a spiritual organisation that transcends religious and ethnic beliefs, with people from all walks of life, from all creeds, religions, professions, nationalities and beliefs coming together to help each other and make this world a better place.

You can seek guidance from books, spiritually enlightened people or even organisations like the one I mentioned in order to find meaning and purpose. In the end, it is your journey of discovery, to find your inner strength or spirit.

GIVE BACK: CREATE A WEALTH OF DIFFERENCE.

Alex Macmillan, who is a very good friend, once told me, 'When I give back to the world what I have been fortunate to earn I always keep this in mind. The best form of giving is to give to those who cannot give back.'

Those words struck a chord in me and I always remember them when I am giving back.

I look at creating wealth as a means to be able to give back to those who are less fortunate. While the saying goes, 'what you give, you get,' if you truly want to give back, you should not expect anything in return because you are giving back what you have already received. That's why I call it 'giving back' and not just 'giving.'

This aspect of creating wealth is in a way connected to spirituality and finding your true purpose in life.

You need to ask yourself these three questions:

- Who are you?
- Why are you here?
- What are you supposed to do?

Now, you have to answer these three questions honestly.

You may not find the answers to these questions immediately. Perhaps it may take you years to find the right answers. Perhaps, even decades or a lifetime, but when you find the answers you will know that they are the right answers.

In order to give something to society, you need to be in a position to do so. If you are constantly engaged in petty jobs trying to make ends meet, you will have no time for giving back. You will neither have time for introspection nor the inclination for finding out your true purpose in life.

It doesn't matter how much or how little you give back. What matters is why you do so. The reasons for doing so should come from within you. It cannot be because it is fashionable or because a religious, moral, ethical or legal code says so.

I often travel the world and work with orphan children to give them a vision of hope by conducting sports and leadership camps. During one of my visits to Africa, I heard a heartrending story, which changed my outlook on life.

I heard this story from a native woman who lived in one of these remote villages in Africa and travelled to another village by foot through a forest for work. After a long day of work, when she was passing through the forest returning home, she heard a noise coming from one of the bushes.

She followed the sound and was aghast to discover a fox chewing on a baby's arm. The baby was crying in pain but hardly any sound came out as it was exhausted. The brave woman drove away the fox and carried the baby with her.

She had no mobile phone or any of the other modern means

of communication we take for granted. Exhausted as she was after a long day's work, she somehow found the strength to carry the baby all the way to the nearest hospital, which was many miles away.

Most of us who live in cities feel proud when we participate in a marathon and complete the 26-mile run. Here was a woman who walked the distance of more than a marathon, at night after a long day's work, and saved a baby's life. And she doesn't even consider what she has done as anything exceptional, but just what was expected.

This story not only transformed my perspective of life but it made me realise how fortunate I am. Whatever amount of wealth I create and however much I give back, I know I will never be able to match what this woman did.

It is stories like these that inspire you to go out into the world and make a difference.

When you WOW Your Way To Wealth, remember the journey is never complete. There is always an opportunity to create a difference in the lives of the lesser privileged around you.

You can only do this if you know who you are, why you are here and what your purpose in life is?

Create your opportunity to do something extraordinary, something transformational. Give and don't expect anything in return. You can do so only when you know you already have created the wealth you wanted to.

Go forth into the world and create transformational experiences.

Start your journey of creating Wealth for Life today, visit www.WowYourWayToWealth.com.

REFLECTIVE QUESTIONS

☞ What did you learn from this chapter?

To give and don't expect anything back. The journey is never complete.

☞ What did you most like about this chapter?

The story of the women who saved a baby's life after a very hard day of work.

☞ How will you apply what you have learnt from this chapter?

Take action. Help people and expect nothing in return.

NOTES

_____

_____

_____

_____

_____

_____

_____

_____

_____

_____

_____

_____

_____

_____

_____

_____

_____

_____

_____

_____

_____

_____

_____

_____

CHAPTER 4

State of WOW

I dream my painting and I paint my dream.

–Vincent van Gogh

When you say, 'WOW!' what do you mean?
You are impressed with something that someone else has done and you express your admiration by saying WOW!

You say it when you are excited about doing something because it is not any mundane or everyday thing. It is something that is not ordinary or boring. It is something that makes you feel good.

You say so when you are enjoying yourself. You are having a wonderful experience. It's aroused all your senses and you want to make the most of this feeling.

It's what the climber feels when he reaches the mountain summit. It's what the runner feels when he reaches the finishing line. It's what you feel when you take a sip of cool lemonade on a hot day.

It's the sense of elation that you get from doing something that you've never done before. It's an expression of joy when you find a spot in a crowded parking lot. It's a sense of belonging you feel when you exchange hugs with family members you are seeing after a long time.

In other words, it involves success, joy, passion, motivation, confidence, ecstasy, love, gratitude and many such positive emotions.

It is an emotional state.

The State of WOW is a state of mind.

It is a state in which you are consistently motivated to do the unexpected.

It could be the state of motivation that helps you generate a great idea for a seminar or workshop, to enable entrepreneurs or businesses to grow.

It could be the state of high energy that makes you deliver a great performance on stage, whether it's a speech, a poetry recital, a dance or just saying a piece of dialogue with sincerity and conviction.

You can tell from the silence and the sense of time standing still that you are in a State of WOW and so is your audience.

It could be the high energy that you feel pulsating through your mind and being after you watch an inspiring movie.

It is the moment of revelation when you can see clearly and truly know in your heart, who you are, what you are meant to do with your life and how you are going to do it.

It is often referred to as the moment of clarity, or epiphany, or inspiration.

Now, imagine living your entire life with this sense of motivation, high energy and inspiration all the time.

This is the State of WOW that differentiates extraordinary people from the rest. This is what makes a sportsperson consistently deliver winning performances or a salesperson successfully close every sales pitch that he or she makes.

You may say it is motivation or confidence or inspiration, or it's just the way some people have all the luck.

It is not luck. It's a deliberately cultivated state of mind. It's what successful people have that others don't.

It's the State of WOW.

Everyone enters a State of WOW now and then. You feel inspired. You feel motivated. You are in a state of high energy and confidence. You know that you can do anything because you believe you can.

Sometimes it is caused by external stimuli. Sometimes it is due to what is going on within you, your inner thoughts, feelings and beliefs.

The question is how can you sustain this energised feeling and sense of confidence always? The answer is to stay in the moment and stay focussed on not just what's happening outside you, but also on what's happening within you.

STATE OF NOW. IS THERE EVER A WRONG TIME?

There is an old Chinese saying, "The best time to plant a tree was 20 years ago. Now is too late but 20 years from now, the best time to plant a tree will be now."

There is no point in having regrets. There is no point in worrying about what will be. Knowing and learning from past experiences and using them to anticipate future outcomes are practical and sensible ways of using your intuition.

The things that you are likely to regret most will be the things you didn't do, rather than the things you did. What will be in the future will surely be influenced by what you do now.

The key to cultivating a constant state of enthusiasm and excitement is to be mindful of the moment, your environment, the people you are interacting with and the emotional and intellectual process that is going on within you.

Carpe Diem. There is no time like the present to do whatever it is that you want to do.

Have you noticed you are always making plans but not putting them into action? Do you put off doing things because you feel you are not yet ready? Do you say you have to practice or prepare or wait for the right time so that you don't fail?

We are all guilty of procrastinating. Not now, later, we say. Dillydallying and coming up with excuses is just a form of hiding your fear.

You have a book within you and if there ever was a right time to write it, it is now.

You are afraid of living in the moment. You are afraid of doing something and failing. You are even afraid of doing something and succeeding because once you succeed you will have no excuse to fail in the future.

Overcoming obstacles, eliminating excuses and doing just what you want to do is simply how you cultivate a constant State of WOW.

ONCE YOU START SUCCEEDING, YOU CAN NEVER STOP.

If someone tells you that something has never been done before, your natural instinct should be to attempt to do it.

It is this sense of stepping into the unknown that drove the explorers to discover new routes and new lands.

In a way, this is what drives entrepreneurs also. It's what makes innovations happen. It's what produces transformational results.

Doing anything for the first time is instrumental to success. Doing something for the first time is to experience the State of WOW.

The outcome doesn't matter. It's the experience that counts.

So, you've never climbed a mountain. Does that mean that you can't? How can you know if something is possible or not without even trying?

So, what if you've never written a book? So, what if no one

else in your family's ever written a book? So, what if you never even thought of writing a book?

Anything you do is how you do everything.

In other words, you can't do some things well and others not so well. You can't make a half-hearted attempt to get up early, sleep in till 10 and then try to hurry up throughout the day trying to finish your tasks and catch up for the time you lost because you didn't make an early start.

You can't write a book if you think you can't.

You can write a book, if you think can.

EVERY MOMENT IS A WOW. IT'S UP TO YOU.

When you think of great people, what pictures come to your mind?

Do you picture them crying? Do you picture them as angry, disappointed or diffident?

Do you see your favourite footballer hesitating to kick the ball? Do you picture your favourite actor having stage fright? Do you picture your favourite comedian in a maudlin mood?

Do you picture Richard Branson cringing with fear when he flies? Most people would consider that blasphemous.

Can you imagine Oprah in a frumpy dress? It would be a crime to even imagine her as anything but elegant, isn't it?

Would you consider Raymond Aaron at a loss for words?

No you wouldn't.

Why? It is because they are all in a constant State of WOW. It's something that comes spontaneously to them. The spontaneity is however, cultivated by years of deliberately doing the best they can.

Have you noticed how when someone yawns, it's infectious and everyone soon follows suit. The person who yawns first is either bored, or he or she had a late night and is tired.

Does that mean that everyone else who follows, who yawns

after the first person yawns, is also bored or sleepy or tired?

No, it's just a behavioural phenomenon. Yawning is contagious. Yawning is however not intentional.

When you yawn, you are unconsciously sending out a signal. It's a sign of boredom or fatigue. It's not a sign meant for others, it's a sign meant for you. It's a way of telling you that you are no longer in a State of WOW. It's a sign that tells you to snap out of it before it becomes a habit.

You yawn when you are bored or tired. You are unconsciously transferring your state of mind to others around you.

Similarly when you are in a State of WOW, you also transmit your sense of wellbeing to those around you. That's how inspirational leaders transform ordinary people to attempt and achieve what they themselves didn't know they were capable of.

So, when you are in a State of WOW, you are extremely enthusiastic, excited, happy and confident. You are fully charged with energy. This energy is transmitted to those around you.

If you are a salesperson, you cannot sell to someone if you are feeling unhappy or if you do not like your customer. You have to enjoy making the sales pitch and you have to be keenly interested in your customer.

If you are a footballer, you cannot score a ball if you see the goalkeeper as an obstacle looming over the goalpost. You have to see the goalpost as being bigger and clearer than the goalkeeper and the other players.

When you are in a State of WOW, you convey warmth and enthusiasm. You create WOW all around you. Whether with colleagues, friends, family or customers, they will see in you an opportunity to create WOW for themselves as well.

Your state of WOW manifests itself outside you and spreads the feeling among those with whom you interact, creating a transformational change in the environment around you, wherever you go.

It naturally flows that the colleagues, friends, family or customers will therefore create opportunities for you to succeed. This is how you attract more opportunities, people, and wealth.

"Some cause happiness wherever they go, others whenever they go," said Oscar Wilde. You can either choose to be the one who makes the sun shine wherever you go or you can choose to be the one who yawns.

The book you write will create a State of WOW even when you are not physically present. Your book conveys your personality and influences the reader. Your book will transmit your energy and enthusiasm to others when they read it because you have poured your heart and soul and all that you believe into it.

Your book is a battery charged with your energy that others can benefit from. Your book is the magic wand to make miracles happen. Your book is a seed you sow now that will enable you to harvest fruits for the rest of your life.

Can you afford not to write it?

Discover how to create your own State of WOW. Visit www. WowYourWayToWealth.com.

REFLECTIVE QUESTIONS

☞ What did you learn from this chapter?

- you must be in a state of wow.
- your state of mind is cruical for success.

☞ What did you most like about this chapter?

- Now is always the best time to start doing the things you want to do!

☞ How will you apply what you have learnt from this chapter?

- Take action.

- change my state of mind.

NOTES

_____

_____

_____

_____

_____

_____

_____

_____

_____

_____

_____

_____

_____

_____

_____

_____

_____

_____

_____

_____

_____

_____

_____

CHAPTER 5

Book Your Words to Wealth

If there is a book that you want to read, but it hasn't been written yet, then you must write it.

–Toni Morrison

What's the one thing that rich people have been telling you but you are not listening?

Write a book.

That's correct. It's not a secret because it's never been kept under wraps. It's a secret because you have not been listening to what every successful person is saying.

Write a book.

When people see you or meet you or hear about you, what is their reaction?

Are they interested? Or are they bored?

Their reaction is a reflection of how they perceive you.

Which do you want to be? Interesting or boring?

When people know that you are writing a book, or that you have written a book, then you are automagically transformed in their eyes.

You go from being boring, to being interesting. You go from being unknown, to unforgettable. You go from being just an expert, to being an authority.

YOU DON'T SELL YOUR BOOK.

When you write a book, you are transacting the information in your mind to someone else, the reader. When you meet and interact with people, you have an opportunity to impart your experience, your wisdom and your insights. When you have written a book, you are able to do so many times over and in a much more organised manner than you could ever do so in any other form.

You have the opportunity to inspire millions of minds and hearts. Your life on this planet is important and meaningful. Don't you want to express what your life means to you?

When you write a book, you have the unique opportunity to connect with potentially millions of people who will read your book. These connections are much more remarkable and memorable than the connections you make on social networking sites or even when you meet someone in person.

Imagine meeting someone and giving them a copy of your book. How will that person remember you? They will remember you as an author.

Now compare this to handing out a business card. Where does your business card go as soon as you leave the room or the scene? If you are lucky it ends up with a whole bunch of other business cards in a rolodex. You are just another 'me-too.' You are just a commodity. You are not a brand. You are not visible. You are not credible. If you are unlucky, your card ends up in the bin.

If you give someone a book, they will not only be taken by surprise because it is not every day that they get to meet someone who has written a book but they will also look at you in a different way.

Do you see how instantly anyone's perception about you changes the moment you give them a book?

Your book opens a new world. The recipient reads your book and then is impressed by the wisdom and knowledge that you are sharing with them through the book.

BECOME AN AUTHOR. BE SEEN AS AN AUTHORITY.

What will someone who receives your book do with it? He or she will read it immediately. Well if they are very busy people then maybe not immediately, but at least at some point when they get the time. Till then they'll keep it on their desk or on their bookshelf where it is visible. They'll probably even carry your book with them when they go from home to work or back again, so they can read it while travelling on the train or when they are waiting for someone at a café.

Do you see the visibility that your book will garner you? Other people will probably ask the reader about your book. Imagine how much your visibility and credibility will increase when the reader of your book says, "I met the author of the book."

While they are reading the book, they will think about you and with every page they turn, their impression about you will change dramatically. You will be transformed into someone who is an authority, who is a giant among ordinary people. You will grow in stature in their minds. You will become credible because you have shared the knowledge and wisdom that was within you with others.

Where does your book put you? It puts you on a stage with spotlights. It puts you on a pedestal. You get noticed because you are interesting.

You go from being unknown to unforgettable.

Your book becomes your marketing tool.

You don't sell your book. Your book sells you.

So whatever it is that you do, whether you are a plumber or a pianist, an engineer or an electrician, a dancer or a designer, you are no longer 'a' plumber or 'a' pianist or 'an' engineer or 'an' electrician or 'a' dancer or 'a' designer.

You are 'the' plumber, or 'the' pianist, or 'the' engineer, or 'the' electrician, or 'the' dancer, or 'the' designer who has written a book.

You are not just an expert. You are an authority.

Anyone can claim to be an expert. If you look around you, everyone who claims to be an expert is either broke or trying very hard to make ends meet.

Your book is better than having a giant big billboard because it conveys much more about you and what you do in a more focussed and classy manner to the people who matter. There will never be another moment when you will be compared to someone who is ordinary, because you have clearly demonstrated that you are a cut above the rest.

YOUR BOOK IS WITHIN YOU.

Did you say you have never written a book? Do you think your friends and family will laugh at you if you tell them you are going to write a book?

Did you say you are not a native English speaker or that it is not your first language?

Did you know that my mother tongue is not English? Did you know that most writers are not native English speakers? No one in my family before me had ever written a book. Therefore, the day I said 'I am going to write a book,' the day I finished writing it, and the day I published it are days when I made history. Of course, there were many who didn't believe me at first and there were many moments when I had self-doubts, but all that changed when I showed everyone my book.

I was transformed. And what transformed me? The book I wrote.

In fact, many times I meet people for the first time and find they already have a copy of my book. That means that they knew about me even before they met me. They tell me that they have read my book or they heard I've written a book from someone else. They tell me how my book helped them transform their lives, lose weight, eat right, live healthy and be happy.

Is there anything better than that? Knowing that you have influenced and impacted hundreds of lives and impressed hundreds of minds is the best reward, and the best return on investment, that I ever received for writing my book.

Two of the most powerful people in the world have my book in their library. One of them is the Queen and the other is David Cameron. And the proof of this is that I received a letter from each of them acknowledging my first book.

I've also received a second letter from the Queen (which makes us buddies, I suppose) with words of encouragement and expressing excitement looking forward to read the second book. So along with you, two of the most powerful people in the world will also have this book.

Now's the time to decide whether you want to spend the rest of your life in obscurity?

Or do you want to be perceived as an authority?

Yes? Then write a book.

How?

That's a good question. You have wisdom. You have knowledge. You have had experiences. You need to share them, but you are so focussed on your work, your career or business that you need guidance and coaching to write your book.

If you write the right kind of book the right way then you will be a brand, and attract more people, more opportunities and more money. But if you write the wrong book, not only will you have wasted time and effort but you can even turn off people and send out a wrong impression.

That's why it is important to know how to write your book

in the right way. Just like when you go on a journey you need to have a clear roadmap so that you don't lose your way.

That's why I have created a simple way that will enable you to write your book in no time. This simple way is a programme created by my business partner and mentor, Raymond Aaron who is himself a New York Times Bestselling Author.

All you need to do is visit www.WowYourWayToWealth.com.

On this website I demonstrate without a doubt how you can write a book in just 10 hours if you want to. But before you do, I wish to list some of the key obstacles in writing a book, and how to avoid them to overcome challenges.

First of all, choose a subject carefully.

You should write about something that people will find interesting and will read. It could be about your profession or your business or your passion. Don't make it into an autobiography or a memoir. You are not so well known and not yet a brand. Your objective is to create your brand. Therefore people are unlikely to be as interested in reading about your experiences as they would be in reading about Richard Branson's, Raymond Aaron's or even mine.

So, while it is not going to be a memoir or an autobiography, it still needs to be written from deep within you. It has to have your own voice but still resonate with your readers. How do you do this? Make your readers a promise that will excite them to read the book. How do you do this? Say it in the title of your book.

This is just the tip of the iceberg.

Seven problems you will face when writing a book.

There are a lot of problems you will face when writing your book, but the seven most common problems are given below.

1. The Foreword

You need someone who is very well known to write a foreword for your book. Why? Otherwise it's very likely that many people will not read your book, even if you have written a great book. That is because you are currently unknown and therefore not credible. When someone who has visibility and credibility writes a foreword for your book, it puts a stamp of approval on your book. The problem is you may end up paying several thousand pounds to someone well known so that they will endorse your book with a foreword. This is a scam. Not only are you paying for something that is insincere but you are most likely not going to get any value from that foreword and therefore all the money you paid for the foreword plus all the effort and time you put into writing the book will go down the drain. How to prevent this? I have a solution for this at my website <u>www.WowYourWayToWealth.com</u>.

2. The Cover

You have heard the saying, 'Do not judge a book by its cover,' but guess what? People judge a book by its cover all the time. That's why you need a professionally designed cover for your book. Otherwise you might have a great book and all the effort will come to naught if your cover does not attract or pull readers to pick up your book. In fact, a poorly designed book cover can actually repel or turn away a potential reader. Getting a professional cover designed for your book may take you many months and set you back a few thousand pounds. This will delay the publishing of your book and also put a strain on your pocket. How to solve this problem? There's a solution at my website <u>www.WowYourWayToWealth.com</u>.

3. Procrastination

This is one of the biggest problems writers face. You may have heard of writer's block. But this can only affect you once you've started writing your book. What if you can't even start because you don't know where to start? That's why you need a book architect who will help structure your book so that it gets written. It's like building a house. If you don't have a blueprint or a plan, you will not know where to start. How to get your own personal book architect? Find out at www.WowYourWayToWealth.com.

4. Publishing your book

Let's say you have written your book. Now what? Do you know how hard it is to get published? It is very hard if you try to publish it the traditional way. It can be very easy and even a liberating experience if you have a powerful publisher who will support you in your endeavour. Don't let your life's work go waste because you can't get your book published. Team up with a powerful publisher who will transform your words into a book and then you can Book Your Words to Wealth. To find out how to publish your book, visit my website www.WowYourWayToWealth.com.

5. Coaching

Just like athletes and sportspeople, no matter how talented they are, need a coach to motivate and guide them, you also need coaching to write a book. Otherwise, you are likely to flounder in the confusion of your own thoughts and doubts. A coach will help you achieve a sense of purpose, clarity of vision and thought, and guide you through the labyrinthine of layers that you need to navigate to see the light at the end of the tunnel. Stay focussed and you will enjoy the task of writing. Get a credible coach who understands just exactly what a first time writer, like you, needs. Go to www.WowYourWay ToWealth.com.

6. Marketing your book

When do you start marketing your book? Once you finish writing your book? This is the wrong answer. You should start marketing your book right now, right away. You should start the moment you decide to write it. Why? Developing a website, marketing materials and channels takes time. You need to get a head start so the momentum you build as you are writing, and the Wow you create as you finish writing isn't wasted. This is just one small tip on how to market your book. Learn plenty of other tricks including how to quickly and effectively have a dedicated website for your book up and running in no time at my website www.WowYourWayToWealth.com.

7. PR expenses

The book that you wrote needs readers. It is just as useful as a door stopper if it doesn't have an audience. To attract an audience you need to create some noise. This is called PR or Public Relations. You will need a grand and glamorous event to launch your book. You will need to invite some well-known people as well as people from the media to this event. How are you going to do this if you don't know anyone? Even this problem can be easily solved. All you need to do is visit my website my website www.WowYourWayToWealth.com to find out.

There is a book within you.

No matter what you think, there's always been a book within you. It is way past time that you wrote it. Now is your time. This is your opportunity to create history, to influence people, impress them and impact lives in a better way.

Are you ready to write your book?

Then go to my website my website www.WowYourWayTo Wealth.com, now.

REFLECTIVE QUESTIONS

☞ What did you learn from this chapter?

There is no better time than now.
Build a brand by publishing a great book.

☞ What did you most like about this chapter?

You are seen as an authority when you become an author.

☞ How will you apply what you have learnt from this chapter?

Follow & copy the steps.

NOTES

"Books are the treasured wealth of the world and the fit inheritance of generations and nations."

—Henry David Thoreau

"You have a book inside you, it's time to get it out"

—Raymond Aaron

"Having authored a book can allow you to reach people you never even dreamt of; even when you least expect it your book will work wonders for you"

—Vishal Morjaria

**To find out how you can effortlessly
write your own book in
the fastest possible time
email info@WOWYourWayToWealth.com**

45358574R00047

Printed in Poland
by Amazon Fulfillment
Poland Sp. z o.o., Wrocław